Biographies
Juan
PONCE DE LEÓN

by Marc Tyler Nobleman

Consultant:
Melodie Andrews, PhD
Associate Professor of Early American History
Minnesota State University, Mankato

Capstone
press
Mankato, Minnesota

Fact Finders is published by Capstone Press
151 Good Counsel Drive, P.O. Box 669, Mankato, Minnesota 56002
www.capstonepress.com

Library of Congress Cataloging-in-Publication Data
Nobleman, Marc Tyler.
    Juan Ponce de León / by Marc Tyler Nobleman.
    p. cm.—(Fact finders. Biographies)
    Includes bibliographical references (p. 31) and index.
    ISBN 0-7368-2667-X (hardcover)
    1. Ponce de León, Juan, 1460?–1521—Juvenile literature. 2. Explorers—America—
Biography—Juvenile literature. 3. Explorers—Spain—Biography—Juvenile literature.
4. America—Discovery and exploration—Spanish—Juvenile literature. [1. Ponce de León,
Juan, 1460?–1521. 2. Explorers. 3. America—Discovery and exploration—Spanish.] I. Title.
II. Series.
E125.P7N63 2005
972.9′02′092—dc22   2003023421

Summary: An introduction to the life of sixteenth-century Spanish explorer Juan Ponce de
    León, who played an important role in the history of Puerto Rico and who discovered
    and named Florida.

Editorial Credits
Roberta Schmidt, editor; Juliette Peters, series designer; Patrick D. Dentinger, book designer
    and illustrator; Kelly Garvin, photo researcher; Eric Kudalis, product planning editor

Photo Credits
Artville, LLC/Jeff Burke/Loraine Triolo, 11
Bruce Coleman Inc./Tony Arruza, 21
Corbis, 12–13; Bettmann, 5
The Cummer Museum of Art and Gardens, Jacksonville/SuperStock, 16–17
Getty Images/Hulton Archive, 20
Houserstock/Dave G. Houser, 14
Mary Evans Picture Library, 7, 18–19
North Wind Picture Archives, cover, 1, 8–9, 10, 15, 22–23, 24, 25

1 2 3 4 5 6 09 08 07 06 05 04

Table of Contents

Chapter 1

Magic Waters

By the 1500s, people had heard many stories about magic waters. Some waters were said to heal sick people. Other waters were said to make old people young again.

People searched for magic waters all over the world. Some people believed there were magic waters in Egypt or India. Other people thought magic waters could be found in France, England, or Belgium.

In the 1500s, Europeans were **exploring** unknown lands. These lands had plants and animals that Europeans had never seen before. Many people thought that these lands might have magic waters.

An artist's painting shows Ponce de León and his men drinking water from the Fountain of Youth.

Many stories say Juan Ponce de León searched for magic waters in 1513. People say he tried to find the Fountain of Youth. These stories are probably only **legends**. But Ponce de León did find Florida. He also made other important discoveries.

Chapter 2

A Spanish Beginning

Ponce de León was born in Santervás de Campos. This village was in the northwestern part of what is now Spain. He was born around 1474.

When he was a young man, Ponce de León joined the Spanish army. At this time, Spanish soldiers fought against the **Muslims**. In 1492, the Spanish defeated the Muslims. With the war over, Ponce de León had to find something else to do.

The next year, Ponce de León heard about Christopher Columbus' **voyage**. Columbus had sailed across the Atlantic Ocean. He had returned to Spain with gold. Columbus also told stories about the land and people he had seen.

The king and queen of Spain welcomed Columbus back from his first voyage. Ponce de León decided to join Columbus' second voyage.

Ponce de León wanted to see the "New World" Columbus found. Ponce de León joined Columbus' second voyage. The explorers sailed from Spain in September 1493.

Chapter 3

The New World

In late 1493, Ponce de León settled on an island. Columbus had named it Española. Today, this island is called Hispaniola. It is home to the countries of Haiti and the Dominican Republic.

In 1502, Ponce de León married a Spanish woman named Leonor. They had three daughters and a son.

From 1502 to 1504, Ponce de León was a soldier on Española. He and other Europeans fought the islanders. The Europeans called these people Indians because of Columbus' mistake. Columbus called the native people Indians because he believed he was in the East Indies.

This map shows what people thought the island of Española looked like in the 1500s. Española was the first place most Spanish explorers visited in the New World.

Europeans
often forced
Indians to
work for them
as slaves.

The Europeans often were cruel to the Indians. They made slaves of some of the Indians. They killed many more. Some Indian groups were completely wiped out. The Indians were angered by the way they were treated. The Indians sometimes attacked the European **colonies**.

As a soldier, Ponce de León helped **conquer** the Taino Indians in Higüey. Higüey was the eastern part of Española. The **governor** of Española made Ponce de León the governor of Higüey. He also gave Ponce de León a large piece of land.

Ponce de León became a rich farmer. He used many Indian slaves to work his farm. They grew **cassava**, sweet potatoes, and other vegetables. The farm also had pigs, cattle, and horses.

People eat the roots of the cassava plant. The roots often are made into flour.

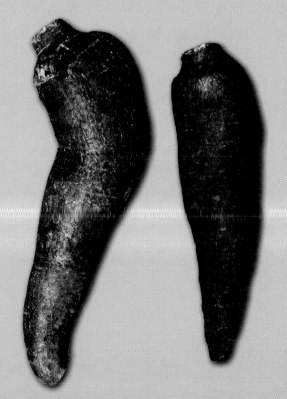

Chapter 4

Puerto Rico and Beimeni

Ponce de León heard Indians talk about great riches on a nearby island. The Indians called this island Borikén or Borinquén. Columbus had landed on the island in 1493. He named it San Juan Bautista.

In 1508, Ponce de León traveled to San Juan Bautista. He found gold and other riches. Ponce de León and his soldiers fought the Indians there. They conquered the island and **claimed** it for Spain.

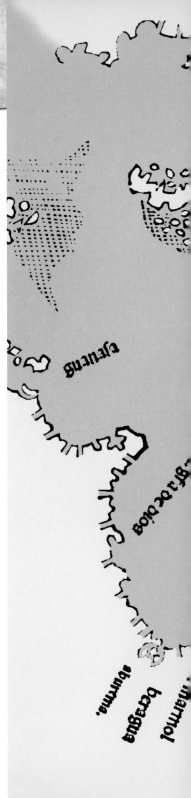

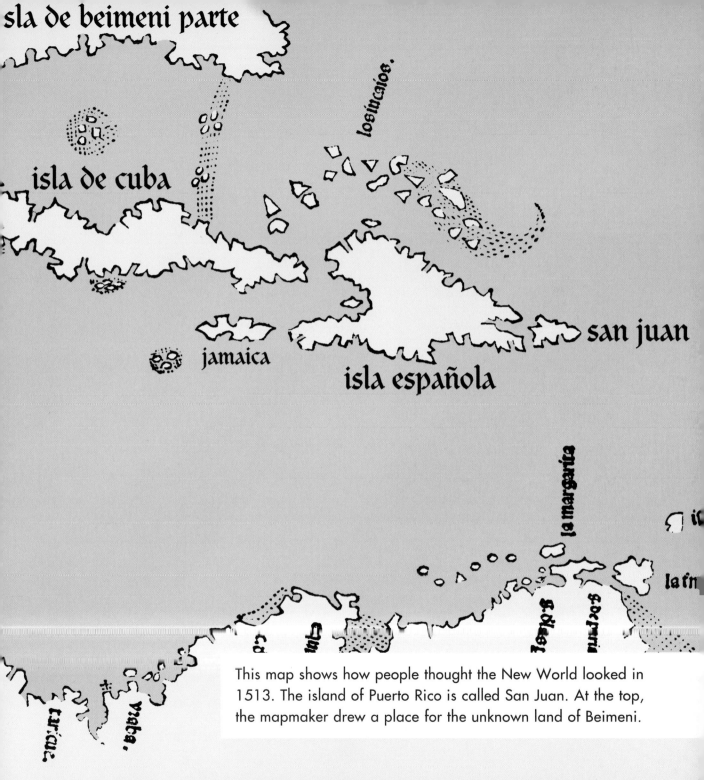

sla de beimeni parte

isla de cuba

loslucaios.

jamaica

isla española

san juan

la margarita

la fn

This map shows how people thought the New World looked in 1513. The island of Puerto Rico is called San Juan. At the top, the mapmaker drew a place for the unknown land of Beimeni.

13

▲ A statue of Ponce de León stands in San Juan, Puerto Rico.

Ponce de León became the governor of San Juan Bautista. Over the next four years, the island became known as Puerto Rico. Ponce de León built the capital city of Caparra. This city was near present-day San Juan. Ponce de León added to his fortune with land, gold, and slaves.

Diego Columbus

In 1511, Christopher Columbus' son Diego went to the king and queen of Spain. He claimed all of the land his father discovered. Diego Columbus became the ruler of Puerto Rico. Ponce de León was no longer the governor.

Beimeni

While in Puerto Rico, Ponce de León had heard stories about an island north of Cuba. The Indians called this island Beimeni. The Indians said that this island had many riches.

In 1512, Ponce de León went to Spain to talk to King Ferdinand. Ponce de León asked for permission to find, conquer, and settle Beimeni. The king agreed.

▲ King Ferdinand of Spain gave Ponce de León permission to explore the land of Beimeni.

FACT!

Most historians agree that the Fountain of Youth was not why Ponce de León searched for Beimeni.

Chapter 5

Florida

Ponce de León left Puerto Rico on March 3, 1513. He was in charge of three ships and at least 50 people. He brought food from his farm for the journey.

Ponce de León and his ships sailed north. They passed through what is now the Bahamas. After a few weeks, the crew saw a long coast. The explorers anchored the ships and went ashore on April 2. They landed somewhere south of present-day St. Augustine, Florida.

Ponce de León believed he had found a large island. He did not realize that he had reached the North American continent.

Ponce de León landed on the
northeast coast of Florida on
April 2, 1513.

Ponce de León claimed the land for Spain. He named it La Florida. In Spanish, *la florida* means "the flowered one." Some historians believe Ponce de León chose this name because he reached the land during the Easter season. Spanish people called this time Pascua Florida, or "Easter of the Flowers." Ponce de León also saw many flowers on the land. Some people believe these flowers were another reason he named the land Florida.

FACT!

In the 1500s, a very large area of North America was called Florida. To the Spanish, Florida was the entire coast from present-day Florida to Canada.

Ponce de León decided to sail around Florida. On April 8, he turned his ships south and moved down the coast. He discovered a strong current in the water. It was like a river within the ocean. Today, this current is known as the Gulf Stream. The Gulf Stream helps ships sail from the Americas to Europe.

Ponce de León and his crew sailed around the southern tip of Florida. They then went around the Florida Keys. Next, they sailed up the western coast of the Florida peninsula.

◄ Early European explorers discovered that Florida had swamps, deer, and alligators.

Ponce de León and his crew met
Calusa Indians along the western
coast. The Calusa Indians did not
want the explorers to take their land.
The Calusas fought several battles
against Ponce de León and his men.

In May, Ponce de León decided to
return to Puerto Rico. He had found
new lands and claimed them for Spain.

▲ Indians lived
in Florida
hundreds of
years before
Ponce de
León arrived.

Ponce de León continued to explore the area as he led the ships home. Ponce de León and his crew sailed south until they reached Cuba. They sailed east along the northern coast of the island. They then turned north and sailed through the Bahamas again. Ponce de León reached Puerto Rico on September 21. His voyage had lasted more than 200 days.

Ponce de León discovered islands west of Florida. He named them the Tortugas. Today they are known as Dry Tortugas.

21

Chapter 6

The Last Voyage

In 1514, Ponce de León sailed to Spain. King Ferdinand honored him for his discoveries. King Ferdinand gave Ponce de León permission to settle Florida.

Ponce de León returned to Puerto Rico in 1515. He was not yet ready to return to Florida. First, he helped fight the Carib Indians. The Caribs did not want to be ruled by the Europeans.

In February 1521, Ponce de León was finally ready for his second trip to Florida. This time, he was in charge of two ships. The ships held 200 settlers, animals, and many other supplies to begin a colony.

The explorers sailed in large ships. They used small boats to get from the large ships to shore.

23

Ponce de León led the ships to Florida and up the western coast. They landed near the home of the Calusa Indians. Ponce de León had fought there on the first voyage.

Ponce de León and the settlers began to build a colony. The Calusa Indians tried to drive the settlers away. During one of the battles, an arrow hit Ponce de León in the leg.

The Calusa Indians fought Ponce de León and the settlers.

Some of the men had to carry Ponce de León back to his ship.

The settlers decided not to stay in Florida. Some of the settlers took a ship to Mexico. Ponce de León and the other settlers went to Cuba.

Ponce de León's wound from the arrow did not heal. Ponce de León died in Cuba in July 1521.

Lasting Impact

Ponce de León was a part of many important events and discoveries in history. He helped the European colony on Española. He started a Spanish colony in Puerto Rico. He named Florida and explored much of the area around Florida. He also discovered the Gulf Stream. Partly because of Ponce de León's work, Europeans began to settle throughout the Americas.

F A C T !

Many places in the Dominican Republic, Puerto Rico, and Florida have been named after Ponce de León. For example, Ponce, Puerto Rico, is named in his honor. Some cities have statues or monuments of Ponce de León.

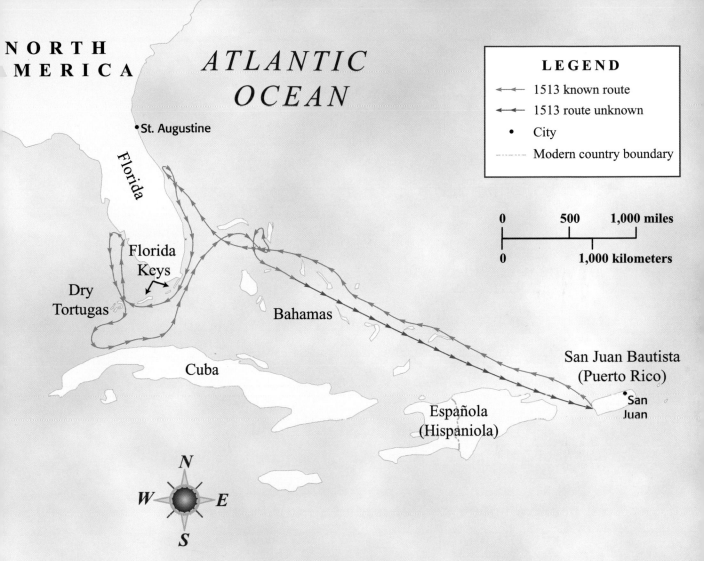

NORTH AMERICA

ATLANTIC OCEAN

•St. Augustine

Florida

Florida Keys

Dry Tortugas

Bahamas

0   500   1,000 miles

0   1,000 kilometers

Cuba

San Juan Bautista (Puerto Rico)

•San Juan

Española (Hispaniola)

N
W   E
S

Juan Ponce de León's First Voyage to Florida, 1513

SOUTH AMERICA

27

Fast Facts

- Juan Ponce de León was born in the northwestern part of what is now Spain.

- From 1502 to 1504, Ponce de León served as a soldier on the island of Española.

- In 1508, Ponce de León conquered the Indians on the island that became Puerto Rico. He served as the governor until 1512.

- In 1513, Ponce de León landed in North America. He believed the land was an island. He named it Florida.

- Ponce de León's crew included a European woman and an African man.

- Ponce de León discovered the Gulf Stream.

- Ponce de León died in Cuba in 1521. He had been wounded in a fight with Calusa Indians in Florida.